THE
BIRCH

Other titles by John L. Peyton

The Stone Canoe and other stories
(1989)

Faces in the Firelight
(1992)

Bright Beat the Water
Memories of a Wilderness Artist
(1993)

for *children*
Voices from the Ice
(1990)

THE
BIRCH

BRIGHT TREE OF LIFE
AND LEGEND

WRITTEN AND ILLUSTRATED BY

JOHN L. PEYTON

The McDonald & Woodward Publishing Company
Blacksburg, Virginia
1994

The McDonald & Woodward Publishing Company
P. O. Box 10308, Blacksburg, Virginia 24062-0308

The Birch: Bright Tree of Life and Legend

© 1994 by The McDonald & Woodward Publishing Company

All rights reserved. First printing, 1994
Printed in the United States of America
by Rose Printing Company, Inc., Tallahassee, Florida

01 00 99 98 97 96 95 94   10 9 8 7 6 5 4 3 2 1

Library of Congress Cataloging-in-Publication Data

Peyton, John L., 1907-
   the birch : bright tree of life and legend / written and
illustrated by John L. Peyton.
      p.   cm.
   ISBN 0-939923-42-4 : $9.95
   1. Birch. 2. Birch — Folklore. 3. Birch — Utilization. I. Title.
SD 397.B5P49 1994
583'.976 — dc20   94-8264
                                                                                    CIP

Credits: "The Student" is reprinted from *Night Watch on the Chesapeake* by Peter Meinke, by permission of the University of Pittsburgh Press; © 1987 by Peter Meinke. The author also gratefully acknowledges permission to quote copyrighted material from Joanne Hart, *Witch Tree*, Holy Cow! Press, Duluth, Minnesota, 1992, and Eino Friberg (translator), *The Kalevala*, Octava Publishing Company, Helsinki, Finland, 1988.

Reproduction or translation of any part of this work, except for short excerpts used in reviews, without the written permission of the copyright owner is unlawful. Requests for permission to reproduce parts of this work, or for additional information, should be addressed to the publisher.

Contents

1   To Light A Fire

7   From Greenland's Icy Mountains

17   Follow My Fire

21   The Birth of Nanabush

27   Sacrifice and Ceremony

37   Gifts of Gods

45   Spare the Rod?

49   Ship and Shelter

59   Art, Literature, and Rawhide

69   Worlds Apart

The Birch Trees at Loschwitz

At Loschwitz above the city
The air is sunny and chill;
The birch trees and the pine trees
Grow thick upon the hill.

Lone and tall, with silver stem,
A birch tree stands apart;
The passionate wind of springtime
Stirs in its leafy heart.

I lean against the birch tree
My arms around it twine;
It pulses and leaps and quivers
Like a human heart in mine.

One moment I stand, then sudden
Let loose my arms that cling:
O God! The lonely hillside,
The passionate wind of spring!

Amy Levy (1861-1879)

THE
BIRCH

CHAPTER 1

TO LIGHT A FIRE

Only will the forest listen,
Sacred birches, sighing pine trees,
Junipers, endowed with kindness,

The Kalevala

His snowshoes catch in a tangle of brush. The woman gives a little hiss calling him back to the trail. He stands there for a moment, searching for the guiding vee of light between the spruce tops. But the short twilight is over and the arc of the new moon is too slim to show the way. They will not get to the cabin tonight.

He tilts back his head to slip off the tump line. The pack crunches into the snow. For a moment he stands there, stretching his muscles, savoring relief from the burden. Then the cold stabs at him through sweat-soaked wool. He stares and fumbles in the darkness. His fingers are numbing in his mittens.

But in this northern forest, what he seeks is never far away. There it is, smooth whiteness catching a little moonlight in the dark wall of spruce. He peels off a strip of bark.

With a snowshoe he scrapes away snow until the wooden rim strikes frozen earth. The woman hands him a bundle of the dead underbranches of spruce. He places the birch bark on the bared spot, builds a tiny tipi of spruce twigs over it. He pulls off a mitten and strikes a match, shielding the small flame from the wind with shivering hands. The edge of the bark shrivels, curls, blackens. Fire runs up the birch and reaches above it to the twigs. The flame brightens, the sticks sizzle. They are damp, annoyed at being broken from the tree, unwilling to burn. The birch insists. The spruce bursts into crackling, spark-spitting anger.

For a few moments the man holds his hands to the heat. Then he pulls on the mittens and unsheathes an ax. The woman has stepped out in the growing light to find bigger wood. In a little while they are sitting in the shelter of a brush lean-to while strips of bacon wrapped around the hindquarters of a hare combine their savory essences on forks of birch sticks propped close to a fire of birch wood.

This couple could be neighbors of yours out winter camping. They could be members of any of the tribes of the taiga, the belt of subarctic forest that encircles the globe. With only small changes in the details of the story, they could have built their fire ten thousand years ago. The alliance between men and trees goes back how long? Seventy thousand years when we stood upright? No, farther than that. Back to when we dropped from the lower branches to take our chances with the other four-leggeds on this dangerous earth? No, of course no; the compact had to be much older than that.

And yet, as recently as the times that I can remember, the woods Indians spoke of a tree as a *who* instead of just an *it*. They respected trees, used them carefully and cut them only after explaining the necessity. In those days, people could still talk with trees and animals.

Most trees are benevolent. Spruce, cedar and willow were especially kind to forest people. But the birch was a sacred tree in North America, Europe and Asia.

The birch was the friend of man, animals and the earth. It flowed into ravaged clearings, holding back erosion until other trees could take root. It gave cover and food to the deer, moose and beaver on whom the lives of the northern hunting peoples depended. It provided shelter, heat and many other blessings for humans. Its buds and catkins, swelling with new life, gave hope in the long and deadly winter.

The word birch comes from the old English *beorht*, bright. A birch branch hung over an English door meant kindness and good health.

Some facts about the birch are solid and practical and can be ticked off neatly. Others are just dim shapes in the mists that hang over rivers, bogs and freezing lakes. These are best expressed in the metaphors of the men and women who moved across those waters and through the forest to find food, shelter and fuel.

When I was young I traveled and hunted with the northern Ojibway, "Birch Indians." The birch tree was as important to them as the buffalo was to the horsemen of the plains.

I'll be speaking of these old friends as they spoke of themselves: Anishinaabeg. An individual male was called an Anishinaabe. An Anishinaabe woman was an Anishinaabekwe. An old-time woods Indian was a gete Anishinaabe. (In the modern written form of Anishinaabemowin, the previously unwritten Ojibway language, a is pronounced as in was, aa as the a in father, and e as in sleigh.)

The Finnish epic poem, *Kalevala*, like *Iliad* and *Odyssey*, is derived from stories handed down by word of mouth through many generations. Lapp and Anishinaabe legends are in the same category.

CHAPTER 2

FROM GREENLAND'S ICY MOUNTAINS

This would be a day to still-hunt.

Ham would climb the ridge that rose against the stars to the northwest. He was fourteen and could be trusted to find his way back to camp. I would walk down the trail to the south and see where it took me.

Ham kicked the burning birch logs of the breakfast fire apart. They would smolder for a while, go out, and wait in their dark circle in the snow, charred, dry, and ready to make quick flame at night.

The black spruce of the swamp stood dark around me but the path ahead reflected a glow in the eastern sky. The light grew stronger. The trail lead up into higher ground. The spruce walls moved apart. I could make out white trunks on both sides. I was in a birch grove.

These trees don't crowd together like the conifers. I could see what was going on for some distance around me. I climbed up on a pine stump and stood there, watching and waiting.

I had been warm beside the fire and while walking, but now I pulled the hood of the parka forward so that its fur ruff closed in around my face. I couldn't hear so well that way, but an old guy has to get comfortable.

It took the sun a long time to clear the ridge and strike the tops of the birches. After that, its level rays soon brought color to the pale trunks. The little flaps of bark, thin as tissue paper, curled out, motionless, eager for the first morning breeze.

The rifle, heavy in the crook of my arm, cramped the circulation so that my left hand was cold in its leather mitten. I was tired of standing. This fresh snow would not squeak or crunch much under foot. I would walk for a while, warm up, maybe find some higher ground with a view over more territory.

I eased down from the stump, took a few steps and saw a burst of antlered gray bound through the birches. I looked along the rifle barrel, had the sight almost on him. The birches hid him for a moment, then he reappeared. Before I could get him in my sights he was gone again. He crossed a vista, just a dark flash in the white trunks and snow. A shorter flash as more trees intervened. Then nothing more. I should have chanced a snap shot. I should have waited longer on the stump.

My son and I were hunting in the evergreen forest that runs across Canada and some of the northern states from the Atlantic to Alaska. East of the Rockies it consists mostly of spruce, but includes pine, balsam, tamarack and cedar. Their heavy foliage shades the earth, so that deciduous trees can't get started. But here and there will be a birch grove, standing light and airy as maypole dancers among a somber majority of disapproving puritans.

Light and airy but not frivolous. These birches are doing an essential job.

Perhaps a half a century ago a fire roared through here, rolling the evergreens in flame. When the fire died, the birches from miles around sent in their paratroops. The double-winged seeds came dropping down in great numbers and secured the area, sprouting quickly to check erosion and to give cover for other trees.

The paper birch is a short-lived tree, lasting not much longer than a human being. It needs lots of light. In northern North America, the conifers are likely to come back to the burned area. A few appear, scrawny little things among the birches, then more, and eventually they grow tall, shade out the other trees, and resume their dominance. The birches hang on, though, numerous in open places and along lakes and streams. Others are scattered through the forest. They brighten the dark spruce background, help deer escape impatient hunters, offer bark to people who need it, and stand ready to repair future damage done by fire, wind or man.

From Greenland's Icy Mountains
To India's coral strand,
Where Afric's sunny fountains
Roll down their golden sand,

The opening lines of that magnificent old missionary hymn may be used to define the range of the birch. From Greenland's icy mountains, yes, for sure, and from Iceland's too. To India's coral strand — well, almost: anyway to India's icy mountains. Where Afric's sunny fountains, no. The birch is not native to any part of the southern hemisphere. The ivory, golden and streaked birches are not really birches, but pale-barked trees of other species misnamed in that cheerfully careless Australian style.

Birches are native to Europe and northern Asia. In Europe and western Siberia, where there are fewer tree species than in America, the birch is often the prevalent deciduous tree, and vast birch forests cover hills and plains.

As the birch moves south into warm countries such as Italy and Spain it keeps mostly to the high, cool hills and mountains. Conversely, when it enters the Arctic prairies it hunkers down into each river valley where there is shelter from the wind and some moderation of the cold by the presence of a considerable body of water. It follows the Mackenzie River almost to the Arctic Ocean.

As you stand on a low ridge beside Hendrik Hudson's bay and look west across the tundra, you feel that, skipping seas, this lovely, formidable monotony of rock, moss and heather must run all the way around the world without a tree.

Maybe it does, but that depends on how you define tree. If you examine the tangled mat of vegetation at your feet you find that it includes some runty tree-things, willow, alder or birch, that crawl along the ground and mingle with grasses, shrubs and caribou lichen to form a flattened forest.

That's a smart tactic because a little farther south where the first spruces dare to stand against the wind, rivers of ice particles come sizzling across the snow surface to sand-blast away their branches leaving clumps of foliage at top and bottom with just bare stick between.

Even there the birches are beginning to raise up a little. The dwarf birch, *Betula nana*, keeps its head down in the

Arctic regions, but may be gnarled and distorted with old age, and very long. It favors swampy places and is found in the tundra and heathlands of Europe and northern Asia as well as of America. As it moves south toward the tree-line it stands higher. It is classified as a shrub, but is tree enough to cross with the paper birch, *Betula papyrifera*, and produce a hybrid that twists its way up to a height of 20 feet or more — undeniably a tree.

When somebody says "birch" in the North American canoe country, he's talking about paper birch. It ranges all the way across Alaska and Canada from the Arctic tree-line south, and over the border into the northern states. It is a medium-sized tree, from 50 to 75 feet in height or sometimes 100 feet. It may be called white birch, canoe birch, or, by poets, the graceful lady of the woods.

The yellow birch, *Betula alleghaniensis*, is a little shorter and considerably stockier than paper birch. It grows in south-

Creeping birch and ice-blasted spruce

eastern Canada and ranges south through Ohio, where it takes to the hills and continues south along the Appalachian Mountains to just touch Georgia. It often lives for 200 years.

The black birch, sweet birch, or cherry birch, *Betula lenta*, is an eastern tree extending from southern Maine south to Georgia and Alabama. It has shiny red bark like a cherry tree and gives off a rich, wintergreen smell when its twigs are broken or its leaves crushed. It's not hard to develop a taste for its buds, just stripped off and chewed.

The river birch or red birch, *Betula nigra*, is found through most of the southcentral United States, west to Texas, up the Mississippi to Minnesota, and north along the Atlantic coast as far as New Hampshire. Its bark color is reddish brown to gray. It grows best in bottom lands and along river banks, where it does valuable service in controlling erosion.

Gray birch, *Betula populifolia*, is a short-lived little tree but good at covering abandoned fields in southeastern Canada, New England and New York, and piles of coal mining refuse in Pennsylvania. When mature it has white bark. It is sometimes called white birch and the yellow birch called gray birch.

The blue birch in eastern Canada and northeastern United States has a couple of Latin names because botanists are not agreed as to its parentage. It's big for a birch, up to 80 feet tall. It has white bark that peels fairly well on old trees.

The little water birch, *Betula occidentalis*, grows in the mountains of the western United States and southwestern Canada. The white birch of Europe and northern Asia is *Betula alba*.

The alder, *Alnus*, is considered a birch by primitive people around the Arctic circle. Botanists classify it as a member of the Betulaceae family but of a different genus from the true birches.

Accepting this official designation (but only for the moment) there are some thirty-five alders. The one I know well, and the one most wide-spread in North America, is the tag-alder, *Alnus rugosa*. It has the horizontal marks, called lenticels, of a birch but is smaller, crookeder and grows in wetter places. An alder thicket may be just a strip of brush along a stream or may extend across a mile or more of flat, wet land, a forbidding place where you must work your way through a mass of crooked trunks, and where your feet keep sinking down between the roots into stinking bog.

If the alder is a birch it is the most cursed birch by hikers, hunters and farmers. It is a get-away place for game birds and animals, and is almost impossible to clear for crop-land or permanent pasture. It is springy and tough to cut and, when it is cut, it grows right back thicker and nastier than ever.

On the other hand, bacteria in alder roots improve the fertility of the soil. Alders will quickly cover a clearcut that is too wet for proper birches. Alders lean out over a creek, shading the water and keeping it cool. If anything can save a trout stream after a tree massacre, it will be the alders.

They also protect mosquito breeding puddles. Alders and mosquitoes are not very good company but they do keep the woods from being overrun by citizens of Minneapolis, Montreal and other great cities of the teeming south.

Shall we call the alder a birch? You can take your choice. I'll stay with the shamans. In my book, that is, in this book, the alder is a birch.

The birch is beneficent but it is not an easy mark. It provides forage for birds and animals. If the browsing pressure gets dangerously heavy, though, the tree may hit back. A chemical compound, papyferic acid, a deterrent to browsers, may be concentrated in the young stems to such an extent that droplets accumulate on the surface of the twigs. Rabbits and caribou don't like that taste.

Birches attacked by the birch borer, a burrowing grub, develop calluses around the diggings and produce toxins. If the tree is healthy it may destroy the invaders. But if it has poor energy reserves, as caused by drought or defoliation, the borers kill a section of the crown. Then, if unfavorable growing conditions continue, the tree will die.

Another of the limiting factors of the paper birch is the forest tent caterpillar. Its natural control mechanisms, like those of the other forest dwellers, are starvation and cold. The caterpillar lives through the winter in an egg mass on the twigs of the trees. Less than 10 percent of eggs are killed at minus 40, but half of them die if the temperature drops to 50 below zero. Thus the cold north is a sanctuary for worm-ravaged birches, and temperature is a limiting factor in the tree's southern range.

Bog birch, *Betula glandulosa*, also known as tundra birch, and dwarf birch, *Betula nana*, are native to most far northern areas of the world. These are small alpine and tundra shrubs commonly known as ground birch. Both species have almost circular leaves, are food sources for birds and grazing animals and thus for hunting peoples.

CHAPTER 3

FOLLOW MY FIRE

*For practice of witchcraft and sorcerie
they [the Lapps] passe all nations of the worlde.*

Giles Fletcher, 1588

The Lapp's best refuge is when he can flee away and hide himself from folk. And that is why the olden time Lapps put their huts under the earth and hid themselves there. The Lapps have had many enemies and amongst others the Ruoša-Tsjuders, who wandered all over Lappland and killed everyone that they found, and took all the possessions that they happened upon. And that is why the Lapps hid silver and money in the earth. The Ruoša-Tsjuders came along on Tsjudebola (Tsjuder-ridge) and the ridge got its name thereby, and it has that name to this day. The ridge ends in a long cape jutting out into the big lake, and there are islands, many islands which deceive you. They are as high as the ridge, and there are many, side by side.

And when the Russians came to the end of this ridge, they met an old woman, and they told her that she must show them the way to the folk. "We will not do you any harm," they said.

And the granny said, "They will be frightened when they see you coming, but if you promise to take me as servant, so that I can make a living, then I will guide you."

The Russians said, "This is a guide for us." So they waited until it was dark, and then the little old mother put on her birchbark coat which was made like this: into it were sewn pockets of bark that held air and they were good for floating with.

So she told them that some of the folk lived on an island, and the others lived on the shore, and she said, "We shall have to wade a little, can you swim?" The Russians said, "That we can." And the Russians asked, "Can you?" "I can a little," answered the old woman.

A north wind came up. And the old woman said, "I will light some birch bark so that you can see to follow me." The Russians agreed to this and promised to help the old woman if she could not hold out with her swimming. And the little mother had a big hood.

And when she saw that the north wind was blowing very hard, she said, "Now we'll go on. The Lapps are asleep, and in this strong wind they won't hear us." And so they set off and swam to the first island. The old woman lighted a big bundle of birchbark. "Follow my fire," she said, and she swam off. And when the bark flamed up the Russians saw it for a long distance and they too set out.

The old woman loosed the bundle of bark and it burnt, and it went on burning, and she loosed her hood too, and the wind carried the fire and the hood far out onto the lake. But the old woman swam behind the islands to the shore. The Russians followed the birch fire. And the wind blew the bark along so quickly that they did not catch it up until they were in the middle of the lake, and then they first caught up the old woman's hood. And when they found it, they said, "She's drowned."

Then they began to search for the way, and swam here and there in the big waves until they could swim no further, and they all drowned there.

Johan Turi as told to Emilie Hatt.

CHAPTER 4

THE BIRTH OF NANABUSH

And Nokomis warned her often,
Saying oft, and oft repeating,
"Oh, beware of Mudjekeewis;
Listen not to what he tells you;
Lie not down upon the meadow,
Stoop not down among the lilies,
Lest the West-Wind come and harm you!

The Song Of Hiawatha, Longfellow

Nokomis, the daughter of the Moon, lived with her daughter on the shore of the big water, 'Tschgumi. One day when the girl was bending to pick berries the west wind blew up under her skirt and into the place of the passage out.

After a while Nokomis could see that her daughter was

pregnant. When the time came for her to give birth, she disappeared in a rush of wind.

Nokomis searched along the lake shore and through the woods. At last she found a clot of blood lying on a piece of birch bark. She folded the bark over the blood and put it away.

Later she opened the package and there was a baby boy. "Grandmother," he said, "I am Nanabush."

Thus was born the god-fool, the man-manidoo, great-grandson of the moon and son of the west wind, creator and savior of the Anishinaabeg, who brought food and fire to his people, who showed them how to build their lodges and their canoes, but who sometimes misused his supernatural power in stupid or despicable ways. A man can feel at ease with that kind of a god.

When Nanabush was almost full grown he stole the magic feathers of the thunderbirds. Then came blasts from the sky. The thunderers were after him. He snatched up the bundle of feathers and ran for his life. Wherever he ran the thunder followed him and the lightning struck around him, closer each time. The claws of the thunderbirds were grabbing at him.

He saw an old fallen birch tree that was hollow. He crawled into it. The claws clicked above him. The thunderbirds shouted, "Nanabush, you have chosen the right protection." You have fled to a king-child. They could not touch him because the birch tree was their own child. He lay there while the thunder rolled away.

When all was quiet again, Nanabush came out of the birch tree and spoke.

"As long as the world lasts, this tree shall be a protection and a benefit to all. If the Anishinaabeg want to preserve anything they must wrap it in birch bark. When people want to take the bark from this tree they must offer tobacco to show their gratitude.

So the birch tree is never struck by lightning. People are safe when they stand under its branches in a storm.

The bark is the last part of the tree to disintegrate. It keeps its form after the wood has rotted away, as it did in the tree that sheltered Nanabush.

The little short marks on birch bark were made by Nanabush but the pictures on the bark are pictures of the thunderbirds.

An Anishinaabe was born in a birch bark lodge, and the birth-smears were washed from his wriggling little body in a birch bark basin. His navel cord was stored for him, with due ceremony, in an ornamented birch bark case. In winter his mother carried him inside a role of birch bark, safe from the driving snow. She weaned him with food in dishes made of birch bark. He sat on a strip of it to slide, laughing and screaming, down snow banks and sand dunes. His first useful work might be picking berries into a small cone fashioned from it. Later he rolled it into a larger cone and called through it to bring the love-crazed bull moose surging through water and muskeg.

He could peel it thin enough to wrap a shell necklace for his love or thick enough to build a thirty-foot war canoe. He could soften it by heat and then bend it into forms that would hold their shape when cool. He could swiftly wrap, twist or bend it into any one of hundreds of useful articles, or carefully and lovingly mold it into a work of art, to be decorated by his wife with beads, quills or with shapes cut from another piece of it.

She would use the bark to make buckets to catch the sap from the maple trees that she tapped as the snow melted in the sugar-boiling moon, and baskets for winnowing wild rice in the month of falling leaves. She stored the sugar, rice, meat, grease and berries in containers made of birch bark and kept them in a cache covered with it. They ate the food with birch bark spoons.

Because of the blessing of Nanabush, food kept better in birch bark than in any other material. When the Anishinaabe traveled to hunt or to make war, a leather bag hanging from his shoulder carried some rice and dried meat in a birch bark container. The flap of the bag would be opened to form an eating place, and then folded back to return any fragments of crumbs to the container.

A broken bone was set by the medicine-man or -woman and then splinted in a piece of heated birch bark that would harden to the exact fit as it cooled.

The Anishinaabe lighted his way through darkness with a flaming birch bark torch, twisted tight to slow the burning. His bark boat carried him over the lake and river road of his life and he carried it over the portages. Chilled, freezing, in tree-cracking cold, he could depend on birch bark to bring him back to life with quick heat, and he could use it to start other fuels burning in a water-soaked or snow-loaded forest.

When he lay sick with fever his wife would cool him with a plain birch bark fan. Men, but only men, might use an ornamented fan. And in the end he would be wrapped and bound in heavy birch bark and buried under a birch bark grave house where that same widow, or a dutiful daughter, would regularly set out a birch bark dish of food for his ghost.

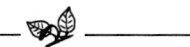

CHAPTER 5

SACRIFICE AND CEREMONY

The groves were man's first temples.
Ere man learned
To hew the shaft, and lay the architrave,
And spread the roof above them ere he framed
The lofty vault to gather and roll back
The sound of anthems in the darkling wood,
Amidst the cool and silence, he knelt down
And offered to the Mightiest solemn thanks
And supplication.

A Forest Hymn, Bryant

This is the place of the birches. The hungry winter is over. The Anishinaabeg have come here for the sacrifice. They have guided their bark canoes through rapids roaring with the frenzy of spring to reach this quiet, holy grove.

Many of the trunks are so thick that two men could not join hands around them. The deeply shaded ground is clear of small growth. The sap flows late in these big trees. Now, when the moon of flowers has slimmed to a narrow curve, the bark will peel in the broad, heavy sheets needed for canoes.

It is time for the annual ceremony that again connects humans with trees. The weegwasoog will gladly give their tough, pliable, waterproof skins to Nanabush's people.

Now the oldest man of the group stands before the oldest tree in the grove. In a quavering but determined voice he speaks the ancient words of gratitude and asks the forgiveness of the trees that would be cut. He begs the spirit of Nanabush's tree to help and protect Nanabush's people. He goes on speaking, very softly now, as he places tobacco at the foot of the birch. The others can see his lips move but they cannot hear this intimate prayer. When he has finished it he offers the smoking ceremonial pipe to the north, south, east, west, sky and earth. The men then join him in smoking as the women light the birch bark under the feast fires.

Early next day they all walk through the grove, admiring and honoring the marked trees. These had been selected, after the custom, in such a pattern that their removal will provide light and space for promising saplings. At each tree chosen, tobacco is offered again to the six points, and a little is placed in the earth between the roots.

The first axman speaks softly and reasonably to his birch, explaining the necessity of cutting it and thanking it for the gift that it is about to make. He chops from one side only so that the butt remains attached to the stump after felling.

His son has placed poles across the fall area to avoid damaging the bark and to keep the trunk off the ground for peeling. He watches with reverence as his father swings the ax.

With reverence, but not without some twinges of doubt. The great tree crashes down, its branches waving like the desperate arms of a falling man. It shudders for a moment, then lies still. Did it hear the prayers and accept the offerings? Did it take that terrible plunge willingly?

The father makes the first cut. He holds the sharp blade at an angle so that knife and bark will be comfortable together. If the knife were to be stabbed straight into the tree, the bark would be angered, grab at the blade and come off with a ragged edge.

A skeptic has wandered off during the ceremony and now comes back eating some berries. He helps the two men pry off the bark with sticks, carefully, so that it will not split. They roll it tightly but gently into compact bundles. As many as a hundred sheets of birch bark are piled in one pack, tied together with basswood strips and carried by a strap on a woman's back to be stored at her home.

The rolls to be used for canoe construction are weighted with stones and placed under water to keep soft until the time comes to stretch the covering over the ribs and hewn planking.

Primitive people were conscious of the cycles of birth, life, and death, and of the sun, the rain and the seasons. They assumed responsibility for taking actions and performing rites that would keep those great wheels turning.

Antal Reguly, a Hungarian born in 1819, was sickly and broke for most of his short life, but he managed to get around in northern Siberia. Working at a time when the old beliefs and ceremonies were still strong, he accomplished more in recording them than did healthier and better financed anthropologists of later years.

One of his Siberian friends was in despair over not being able to offer a horse to Palm Tarum, the god that lived in a birch grove. He felt sure that something bad would happen to him or to his family.

Reguly managed to get together enough money to buy a colt. The shaman decided that yes, that could be counted as a horse. The god stood on an almost-horizontal birch branch and watched the ceremony. A horse feast followed.

A carpet of birch twigs was spread under the stone where a reindeer was to be sacrificed.

The Anishinaabeg had no horses and no tame reindeer but they had dog sacrifices followed by dog feasts. In Europe, at an earlier time, both animals and people were sacrificed.

In the European and Asiatic pine forests, north of the range of other deciduous trees, birch buds told the people that life continued through the winter. When they cut a birch sapling it would sprout again as a cluster of birches. Clearly, this was the tree of births and beginnings, the symbol of self-propagation.

There were thirteen letters, all consonants, in the tree alphabet, passed by word of mouth from the Druids down through the centuries. (The vowels came later.) The birch was *beth*, B, the first letter. These consonants also form a tree-magic calendar of thirteen twenty-eight-day months, plus a day. The first or birch month extended from December 24 to January 21.

Birch rods were used to beat and drive out the old year. In Ireland a child's first cradle had to be made of birch wood, in Siberia of birch bark. The birch was used by Romans as a tree of inception during the installation of the consuls, which also took place in the spring. In Scandinavian mythology, too, the birch was consecrated to Thor, and symbolized the return of spring. Thor was the thunder god. As in North America, the birch offered protection from lightning.

When the birch put out new leaves the financial year began in England and the agricultural year in Norway and Sweden.

Birch was given as the April 14 birthday plant with the sentiment of grace and meekness. In the language of flowers it meant: you may begin. When given by a woman to a man it was a sign of encouragement.

Siberian *sos* dolls were made from the inner bark of birch and were kept in a pregnant woman's sewing bag, so that the child would not be too big and the delivery would be easier.

The *sos* was used by the attending shaman to predict the nature of the birth, and, in case of a difficult or late delivery, to find out what the trouble was. A dress was made for the mother from the birch-charmed sewing materials to be worn during the first week after the birth. Later this dress was left in a birch bark bucket in a remote part of the forest where it would be unlikely to contaminate a man.

In all the northern countries the bear's fat meat provided a valued and needed addition to the lean diet of winter. A successful bear hunt was the occasion for a joyful feast. The bear was the symbol of renewal among animals as the birch was among trees. The killing, dressing and eating of a bear had to be done with the proper ceremonies.

Women had an important part in these rituals in recognition of the miracle of birth, of life coming out of the womb as the bear and her new cubs came from the winter cave. Birch and alder were also essential. The blood of the bear, menstrual blood, and sap, the blood of the tree, were all part of the mystery. The Lapp word for alder is the same as for bear's blood and menstrual blood.

In Lapland and Siberia the dead bear was sprinkled with alder bark juice, then dragged back to camp. The shaman in charge of the ceremony was called the alder man.

Among the Samoyedes of northeastern Siberia the man who had killed the bear would beat three times with a whip plaited of birch twigs at the entrance of the tent. He then struck the dead bear with the whip to help it back toward life, just as children were wakened on Easter morning by a gentle tap with a birch twig. It was believed that the life force was inherent in the budding branch and could be transferred to other beings.

The hunter handed over the birch whip to the women, who wrapped it in linen cloth and decorated the bundle.

When the hunters returned to their village with a slain bear, Obugurian women surrounded the carcass, holding out smoldering birch tinder in a purification ceremony.

Lapp women spat alder-bark juice at the hunters through a brass ring. They sprinkled the bear and the dogs with the alder-spittle protection and also the reindeer that dragged in the bear and the children that brought the meat to the women.

In both Lapland and Siberia a birch bark cone filled with chewed alder bark was placed before the dead bear's nose. The muzzle of the bear might be buried in this cone. In the American forest, men ate the muzzle, but no Anishinabeque was allowed to touch it.

When a Samoyede bear-banquet was over, the bear's vertebrae were threaded on the plaited birch whip in their natural order and then buried together with other bones so that the bear might come back to life. American Indians followed a similar procedure.

In Greek mythology the dryads or wood nymphs wedded to the birch were represented as melancholy, fragile young women with floating hair. In Finland, the origin of the birch was attributed to a maiden's tear. To the people of Estonia the birch tree was the personification of their country.

The Sioux, enemies of the Anishinaabeg, burned small pieces of birch bark as protection against the thunderers.

The birch tree is pictured on the sacred drums of Siberian tribes.

The birch cleanses. Steam bathers in Finland and Russia slapped themselves and each other with *vasta*, bundles of birch twigs tied at the butt end with birch withes. When steeped in hot water these gave off a sharp, clean, medicinal odor.

This cleansing was efficacious against more than just ordinary human dirt. Evil spirits too were washed away.

"Besom brooms" made of birch twigs were used in England for cleaning out a bewitched property. But the supernatural underworld finds ways of turning to its own uses the implements of law and order. Witches discovered that some of the bad spirits became entangled in the twigs. A witch who secured one of these polluted brooms might bind the birch sticks to an ash handle to make a broomstick on which she could ride across the country in carrying out the duties of her profession. The ash protected her against drowning, a fate to which witches were particularly susceptible.

Christian peoples of the far north believed that the birch of the Arctic prairies lay low along the ground out of shame for the birch rods that were used to scourge Christ. In Newfoundland it was considered unwise to make birch brooms in May, for they might sweep a family away.

The dead were wrapped in birch bark by Siberian tribespeople just as they were by the Anishinaabeg. In Scotland, birch was associated with the wraiths of those who appeared to the living after death. In the ballad, *The Wife of Usher's Well*, the dead sons return to their mother in the winter with hats of birch. Those were taken from a tree beside the gates of Paradise, a sign to the living that these ghosts will not haunt the world but will return to their heavenly home.

Robert Graves, in *The White Goddess*, presents thoughts and studies on the Druidic alphabet and on the birch in folk lore. He connects the birch month, Beth, with *Betulus*, the Latin word for birch, which he transliterates into Greek as *Baitulus*. From this point he traces an intricate but convincing trail to two goddesses, *Ashima Baetel* and *Aanatha Baetyl*, who were Jehovah's wives according to a Hebrew cult of the fifth century BC.

Not every reader in this television age will be sufficiently versed in Greek, Latin and Hebrew to make the most of Graves' text, but the family connection between the stern god of the old testament and the easy-going religions of the north is worth noting.

> *Nature is a temple where living pillars*
> *Sometimes let out confused words.*
> *Man passes through forests of symbols*
> *Which observe him with a familiar gaze.*
>
> *Fleurs Du Mal*, Beaudelaire

Chapter 6

Gifts of Gods

Said the eagle, bird of air:
Excellently you have managed
To have left this birch tree growing,
Left this graceful tree upstanding

The Kalevala

Hikers in the Italian Alps noticed somebody's head sticking out of a glacier. When chipped clear he proved to be in good condition for his age (5300 years). His gear included two birch bark cups that looked as solid and efficient as though they had been stitched by an Anishinaabekwe.

So the birch has been used for a long time by humans, and in the south as well as in the north. It is admired as an ornamental tree for lawns and parks in most of the world. It is useful, plentiful and profitable throughout the northern hemisphere. In the tundra and the boreal forest the birch made survival possible.

The American section of these subarctic regions resembles the Eurasiatic section in its animals, vegetables, minerals and bugs. Canadian birches are only a little different from birches on the other side of the pole. You could hardly tell the difference between the Siberian "elk" and the moose that we summoned to our rifles with birch bark cones. The birch bark lodges along the Yenisie River looked much like those on the Coppermine. To the Lapps, Finns, Samoyedes, Kotyaks and Chukchi, to name only a few of the Eurasian peoples, as to the Anishinaabeg, the birch was the tree of life and legend.

Birch is also an important forest product to modern man. It is used for flooring, interior trim, doors, plywood, pulpwood and furniture. It is the principal firewood in Scandinavia, Finland, northern Russia and Siberia. It rots quickly if exposed to moisture, but, treated with preservatives, it can even be used for railroad ties. In northern Europe and Asia the bark is used for roofing. The aromatic oil of some species of birch is extracted and used for flavoring and in medicine. Birch is impervious to water and, for this reason, the wood is used locally in northern Europe and Asia for roofing shingles.

Twigs and bark of *Betula lenta*, combined with honey, are fermented to make a very strong beer. In the spring, birches can be tapped like maples. The sap is only about half as sweet as maple sap, so it takes a lot of boiling. But the birch produces more sap than maple does, and some epicures consider the flavor better than maple.

The gete Anishinaabeg said that stew cooked with hot stones in a birch bark container tasted better than the same stuff cooked over a fire in an iron kettle.

In 1842, before the forests of Scotland were conquered by sheep, an English visitor wrote about the uses to which highlanders put the birch. "They build their houses, make their beds and chairs, tables, dishes and spoons, carts, plows, harrows, gates and fences, and even ropes of it. The branches are employed as fuel in the distillation of whiskey. The spray is used for smoking hams and herrings, for which last purpose it is preferred to every other kind of wood. The bark is used for tanning leather, and sometimes, when dried and twisted into a rope, instead of candles. Birch twigs are placed at the bottom of cooking pots while making soups or stews to prevent the meat from sticking to the bottom and burning."

Birch shoes were standard footwear for the poor in medieval northern Europe. A farmer clearing land for pasture is likely to leave a few birch trees because the slender trunks take up little space and the light foliage gives shade for cattle without being so dense as to kill the grass. Sheets of birch bark were used as roofing, often overlaid with sod.

My own memories of the birch are intimate and grateful. The wood is strong but takes a clean cut. A few minutes of ax work provided birch poles and pegs for the tent, forked sticks for cooking, and the "dingle stick," a heavier piece to be wedged and weighted with rocks for suspending the kettle.

No matter how rain-soaked the forest, a strip of birch bark would kindle a fire. Wood from a dead but sound standing birch burned with a hot, bright flame that was just right for cooking. It was easily controlled by pushing the burning pieces together for more heat or pulling them apart for less. It soon made good coals for roasting or baking. But if you were too hungry to wait for the coals you could impale your meat or fish on a forked stick of green birch and broil it close to the flame. Unlike the evergreens, birch refrained from shooting sparks into wet socks hung near the fire to dry.

Sometimes we'd bind two birch sticks upright in a canoe to hold a tarp up as a sail. (Before canvas, the Indians used birch bark.) Without some kind of a keel or sideboards, a canoe can't sail into the wind, but when you and the wind happen to be going in the same direction you get a rollicking ride.

The Anishinaabeg shaped birch bark for cups, bowls, baskets and trays by heating the bark and then bending it to the shape needed. It would keep that shape when it cooled. Folds were pierced and sewn together with basswood bark or spruce roots. When a watertight container was needed the seams were caulked with spruce pitch. All these birch bark vessels were surprisingly strong, considering their light weight. Food was said to keep better in them than in containers made of any other material. Berries and corn were dried on sheets of birch bark. Blankets, supplies and equipment were wrapped and bound in birch bark mats for the long and frequent moves of the canoe nomads.

I am told that the Anishinaabeg used to cook with birch bark containers over a fire. If so, that skill had been lost by my time. The cooking was usually done in iron pans and kettles but when these were not available stones were heated in a fire, removed with tongs of green wood and dropped into a birch bark bucket that had been partly filled with water.

It was also said that the gete Anishinaabeg could take bark from small or medium size birches at a certain season without hurting the tree. That, too, I have to take on faith. Ordinarily, stripping bark leaves a permanent and unsightly scar on the trunk and exposes the tree to insects and disease.

Other Indians at one time probably depended on the birch to as great an extent as did the people I knew. Anthropologists speak of the Old Birch Bark Hunting Culture of the northeastern tribes. Part of this culture were sea-hunts

Container, moose call, and shoes of birch bark

for whales, carried out in big birch bark canoes. In New England, especially in Maine, the Abenaki had access to the bark of tall, broad birches but their culture had been subject to more pressure from white civilization and they had forgotten many of the old ways.

The Montagnais and Nascapi of Quebec made good use of the bark. So did the now-extinct Beothuk of Newfoundland. The birch tree and its bark were important to the Swampy Cree of northern Ontario, the Forest Cree of Manitoba, all the western forest tribes and the Athapascans of northwest Canada. But farther north, as we have seen, the birch dwindles in size. Its bark is thinner there and has more knots. So the northern and western people had to work with smaller, thinner and rougher sheets of bark than did the Anishinaabeg.

Clear, dry northern air allows strong sunlight to shine down at the time of year when the sun hangs low in the south all day, glaring up

Birch bark mask to prevent snow-blindness

from the surface of the snow into the eyes of anyone following the frozen waterways. To avoid being temporarily blinded it is necessary to wear some sort of goggle. In Siberia and North America, before dark glasses came in, masks were made of birch bark with slits cut just wide enough to let the wearer see, or cut in half circles, heated, and bent down to protrude beneath the eyes, giving protection with full vision.

In all the circumpolar lands north of the tree line dwarf birch was used for arrow shafts and mats. It is still an important fuel in that almost woodless country.

The thickness of a piece of bark determines the use to which it is put. The "spring-peeled" bark, often referred to as winter bark, is heavier and harder to remove than the summer bark, but very durable. That coming from the largest trees has from six to nine layers and is strong enough to be made into canoes and lodge coverings. Some of the bark is as thin as tissue paper and tough enough to use for wrapping packages. The Anishinaabeg gathered the bark from the time the leaves of the birch tree unfolded until the end of July before it was set and while it could easily be peeled.

North of the range of maples — and that includes most of Canada — birch was the strongest and hardest wood available for implements. A birch sapling would be bent and triggered against a notched stump to hoist a snared hare into the air, beyond the reach of foxes. Bowls, toboggans, ax handles, bows, arrows, spears and snowshoe frames were made of birch. Birch paddles were heavier than spruce, but stronger. Farther south, bowls and pestles for grinding corn meal were made of birch.

The birch was widely used in folk medicine and was regarded as a safeguard against wounds, gout, barrenness, caterpillars and the evil eye. The Catawba Indians boiled the buds of the yellow birch to a syrup, added sulfur, and made a salve for ringworm or sores. In Newfoundland the inside bark of the birch was applied with cod liver oil to cure frostbite. A distillation of birch leaves was used to break kidney stones and wash sore mouths. For difficult labor the Anishinaabeg medicine-men and -women prescribed a decoction of scraped alder with dried bumblebees. They boiled and crushed the inner bark of the birch for a poultice on wounds and burns. They heated the cones of the dwarf birch to make incense for patients suffering with catarrh. Alder bark was used to cure colic, diarrhea and vomiting. Further south, the bark of the black birch was steeped in water to get a cure for stomach pain.

Many of these old Indian remedies have been taken over by white medicine people and form an important part of our present-day *materia medica.*

Cunningly the girl replied:
"Maybe I will come when you
Peel off birch bark from a stone..."

The Kalevala

CHAPTER 7

SPARE THE ROD?

When I began to peel a birch rod
She caressed me as her birdling

The Kalevala

Useful as was the birch to primitive people, one of its greatest contributions was in the encouragement of good behavior in civilized Europe and America. It was used to accomplish these advances by the enforcement of civil, academic, ecclesiastic and family discipline.

Finnish authorities, as noted below, recommended just showing the birch to the disobedient party before using it.

Often that would be enough. But even the fondest father or husband occasionally had to apply the rod.

> *Now, as fond fathers,*
> *Having bound up the threatening twigs of birch*
> *Only to stick it in their children's sight*
> *For terror, not to use, in time the rod*
> *Becomes more mocked than feared.*
>
> *Measure for Measure*, Shakespeare

The birch was the traditional instrument used by the state to punish unruly citizens, by the church to convert the heathen, by citizens to correct disobedient wives and children, and by teachers in the instruction of the young.

When the kings had been driven out of Rome, the Patricians brought to reason and the one-man-one-vote principle established, the symbol of government was the fasces, a bundle of birch rods tied around an ax. Thus the Tribunes of the People could punish with flogging, or, if necessary, with beheading, anyone who might attempt to overthrow the new democracy.

The rods and ax, emblem of populism, was taken over by Mussolini and made a symbol of despotism, just as the swastica, an ancient and honorable good luck sign commmon to Europeans, Asians, and American Indians, was seized and debased by the Nazis.

Until recently, the supple birch was considered essential to the education of an English gentleman. In British schools, "birch" was both noun and verb. Wellington said that Waterloo was won on the playing fields of Eton. If so, the products of those fields could hardly have gained victory had they not, in their formative years, been properly birched.

In rural American schools the erring pupil would be sent out to cut the birch to be used on himself.

The *Kalevala* and its Ojibway oral counterpart, the Aadizookaanag, both mention the birch often and respectfully. Both are designed to induce good behavior but in one important respect they differ. In Anishinaabe legend the uppity woman was punished with ridicule. In the birch bark lodge she was simply ignored. It was unusual for a gete Anishinaabe to strike his wife, child or friend.

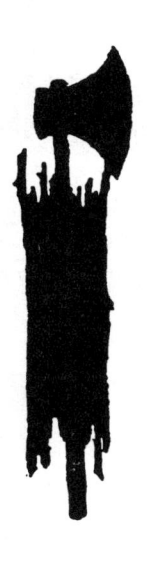

In Runo 24 of *The Kalevala*, bride and groom are given explicit instructions on their behavior to insure a happy marriage.

The husband must be gentle and forgiving with the wife. He must never strike her with a club or knout. If she absolutely refuses to obey, he should cut a little birch rod from a woodsy hollow and show it to her, brandish it politely over her, but don't hit her yet. Even if she still holds out, he is instructed not to proceed with punishment out in the open where the nosy neighbors are probably watching.

He must take her into a tightly-chinked cabin where her weeping will not be heard by gossips. There he is to switch her on the back and buttocks, never in the face. She must not have visible welts that would cause other women to laugh at her.

By present standards, such punishment, or any physical punishment, would be outrageous. In medieval society it was a great step forward. The substitution of the birch switch for the club was a necessary precursor to all the later advances in women's rights.

In those more honest and manly ages, prisons were little used except as warehouses for prominent people being held for ransom. Common folk were not held long in the small gaols, but were corrected, as in ancient Rome, with the birch or the ax.

In our time of great, overcrowded prisons, overviolent society and an overpopulated world, the old criminal justice procedures would have certain advantages. And a little birching again in school might prepare our youth to meet the next Napoleon.

CHAPTER 8

SHIP AND SHELTER

*... of a very elegant form ... so light and slender
that one wonders how they can carry five or six people,
their dogs, their tents, and all their moveables.*

J. C. Beltrami, 1828

This is a stable little unit in a changing expanse of time and space. The scenery shifts from a dawn-bright path over the dark surface, to misty river, to swamp, to open lake but the cedar thwart stands solid and still in front of the man in the stern. Beyond the thwart, the children's heads protrude, quiet among the packs and boxes. The bow paddler's shoulders move, but always in the same steady rotation. She sets the pace with short, quick, efficient strokes. Only her kerchief changes, fluttering as the first morning breeze moves over the river.

The sun burns away the mist and reflects up from the water. The man in the stern pulls off first his jacket and then his shirt. He watches the back of the bow paddler's dress darken with sweat but she holds the pace.

Portages are hardly an interruption. Everyone carries a pack. The canoe rides bottom-up on the man's shoulders. Sooner or later the next water gleams through the trees. Cargo and passengers are quickly back in place and the paddles are moving again.

All day the liquid miles flow beneath them, cooling the kneeling and sitting bodies through the thin hull. At night, camp is made quickly. Each person is familiar with his or her duties. The canoe is placed on its side and tilted forward as a shelter, supplemented by a sheet of birch bark in rainy weather.

The family is afloat again at daybreak. They cross broad areas of bog, pass beneath cliffs, pole and portage up steep rivers, carry over a divide, and run rapids. In the white downhill surges and wind-tossed lakes, the canoe comes to life, flexing its springy cedar ribs and tough birch bark skin to find safe passage around boulders and rise above waves.

Birch canoes carried a family or a group of families over these waterways to gather meat, fish, rice, maple sugar and berries, to harvest each crop at the right time and place and to store it against the winter's threat of starvation. A bark canoe with a capacity of almost a ton of cargo could be carried over portages by one person. A war party would travel in swift, silent canoes to strike the enemy.

The first Europeans to sail into Canadian harbors looked down from their decks with wonder at the agile little boats that came circling around them. When they lowered their own longboats these were unable, even with many oarsmen, to keep up with two-person canoes.

> These . . . go as swiftly as may be without sails; when they move they put all they have into them, wives, children, dogs, kettles, hatchets, matachias, bows, arrows, quivers, skins, and the covering of their houses.
>
> They are made in such sort that one must not stir nor stand up in them, but must crouch or sit in

the bottom, otherwise the merchandise would overturn. They are four feet broad or thereabouts in the center and grow narrower toward the ends, with a high prow in order to pass easily over waves.

Building a canoe

I have said that they make them of bark, to keep which in shape they garnish them with circles of cedar, a wood very supple and pliable, whereof Noah's ark was made; and to the end that they leak not, they coat with the gum of fir trees the seams where the said pieces of bark are joined together, which is done with roots.

Mark Lescarbot, about 1605

European explorers, with Indian guides, went in bark canoes from the Gulf of the St. Lawrence up the great lakes and down the Mississippi to the Gulf of Mexico, through the tundra to the Arctic Ocean, and across Canada to the Pacific. The Anishinaabeg and other Algonkian tribes brought furs to

Montreal by canoe until the powerful and deadly war parties of the Iroquois, also canoe-borne, cut off that trade.

The white fur traders came next, by canoe. The legitimate permit-holders, restricted by tight government regulations, were often out-competed by *coureurs de bois*. The woods-runners had learned that, in this country, Indian in-laws were more important than King Louis' laws. Eventually most of these free traders became voyageurs, canoemen employed by the fur companies to man the north canoes that penetrated the back country, or the great *canots du maitre*, 36 feet long, that brought supplies from Montreal and carried the furs back.

> With their short tobacco pipes in their mouths and their children in wooden cradles on their backs, my women dragged young trees from the wood and thrust them into the ground at equal distances, so as to form a quadrangle....
>
> When the tall young trees are fixed in the ground, and stand perpendicular like a basket maker's framework the side branches[1] are bent down and fastened together two and two, when their ends are twisted round each other and secured with bast. For this purpose the extremely tough bast of the Canadian cedar is used....

---

[1] There is something wrong here. The vertical poles, not the side branches, are bent down and fastened together. This is probably a translator's error.

Thus the carcass is completed; but to give it greater firmness and allow the covering to be put on, crossbars are added. These are young trees or branches laid horizontally along the trellis work and firmly tied at all points of intersection. The whole then resembles a widely laced basket of semi-oval form.

Although my women were busy enough after their fashion, I had no occasion to warn them against injuring their health with excessive toil. Besides building, they had many other matters to attend to; at times the old woman's pipe would go out, and she ran into the nearest hut to relight it. Then a small boy came up whose shirt was unfastened, and his clothes had to be tied up with a bit of the same bast employed on my mansion. Then they must look tenderly at their children whom they had propped up against the trees, run and kiss them, put their hands, ribbons, or caps straight, or sit down for a minute in the grass, lost in admiration of the little one.

While I was considering all this, the apakwas had arrived and my house-skeleton was about to be clothed. This is the name given to the rolls of birch which are generally kept in readiness to cover the wigwams or repair the roofs. These consist of a number of large quadrangular pieces of birch bark sewn together. Each piece is about a yard square, for a larger piece of birch bark, free from flaws and branch holes is rarely met with. Six or seven such pieces are sewn firmly together with cedar bast and then formed into rolls resembling the cloth in our tailor's shops. That these rolls may acquire greater stiffness, thin laths are sewn into each end of the strip, on which they may be comfortably rolled while the end most exposed to contact is covered with a double piece of bark, and the roll tied round so as to be easier of carriage.

The women have always some of these rolls ready to hand, and hence I was able to purchase the nine or ten I required, or the bark of some sixty trees, from my neighbors. The women began covering the hut from the bottom and bound a couple of round apakwas round it to the branches: the second row hung down over the first so that the rain would run off it: and third and fourth row completed the whole, and a couple of apakwas were thrown crossways over the hut leaving a smoke hole in the center. A mat was hung over the space left as a doorway.

In order that the wind might not disturb the apakwas, long cords of bast were thrown across, with the heavy stones fastened to the ends. In this way the semiconical wigwam was completed, and received the due amount of firmness.

Kitchi-Gami, Life among the Lake Superior Ojibway,
Johan Georg Kohl, 1855

The winter wigwam might be cone-shaped, rather than Kohl's semiconical or domed structure. Where several families came together for winter hunting, the ground plan of the lodge would be lengthened from circular to oval to make a long house.

Farther north the floor was likely to be dug down below the surrounding ground level. The lodge would be reinforced with heavy timbers, double-walled with bark, further insulated with moss and forest duff, and finally banked with snow.

The bark houses of Minnesota Sioux could house ten or fifteen people. Their vertical side walls have been thought to indicate white influence. But there were vertical walls in the Iroquois birch bark long houses described by Champlain and other early explorers.

As the Sioux were driven west, skin coverings took the place of bark. Along the southern range of birch, elm or rush bark mats were used for the vertical sides of the domed lodges, with birch bark overhead to turn the rain.

As with most other details of woods Indian culture, the lodge changed with the advance of European customs, not always for the better. Canvas took over gradually. Wigwams would be part bark, part canvas, and, later, all canvas. When the trees had been clearcut and canvas was unaffordable, the lodges were covered with tar paper, a terribly inadequate material for northern winters but better than nothing.

CHAPTER 9

ART, LITERATURE, AND RAWHIDE

A further guard would be that one of these copies [of the daily records] be on the particular membrane of the paper birch as less liable to injury from damp than common paper.

Thomas Jefferson in a letter to
Captain Meriwether Lewis, June 20, 1803

Jefferson's instructions to his expedition's leader did not represent one of the progressive President's entirely new ideas.

The word "library" comes from the Latin *liber*, book, whose root meaning is bark. According to the historian, Pliny, the books of Numa Pompilius, one of the earliest kings of Rome, were written on birch bark. The same writing material was used by the New England colonists. Birch bark was the customary material for documents from 800 to 1700 in Russia, and was preferred there even later for important records because of its durability. It has been called vegetable rawhide.

The Anishinaabeg used birch bark for maps, to convey messages by pictures and symbols, and to record time, past events, dreams, songs, rituals and stories. The birch bark scrolls of their mysterious Midiwewin Society were mnemonic, intended only as reminders for the initiates, not for readable documents. Secrecy had to be maintained to foil thieves who might try to steal the magic power of a song or ceremony and also to keep the supernatural power from leaking away.

I pushed from dark woods through fallen timbers and raspberry vines into a clearing where several winter cabins basked in the sun. A bear rose up out of the brambles, looked me over, then hustled two cubs into the safety of the forest.

Fastened to the door of one of the cabins was a birch bark scroll marked with a strange assortment of triangles, lines and circles. This was a message left for someone, but I could make nothing of it.

Thus I was introduced to a kind of writing known as syllabics This system, devised by missionaries, has been widely accepted by the Cree and northern Anishinaabeg for use on birch bark. The sounds of different syllables are indicated by a logical sequence of lines, curves, triangles and circles, providing a more exact and more easily remembered means of pronunciation and communication than does an alphabet. Some woods Indians still feel more at ease in writing syllabics than in either English or Anishinaabemowin.

As we come to the subject of the birch in art, the first thing to consider is the birch itself as a work of art.

Wherever landscapes have been painted in the birch's range, it has been one of the most frequently depicted trees. It is at its best when standing against a background of its dark conifer neighbors, especially when spilling its reflection down on trembling water, or bending in a swirl of snow. Its pale bark and swarms of lacy twigs that rise like a fountain on slender but strong branches, give it a feminine delicacy and seeming fragility, along with the basically sturdy structure that underlies the loveliness of trees and women.

Gerry Peirce, who came from Arizona to teach watercolor in northern Minnesota, said that our birches reminded him of little nude dancers.

My favorite time to paint birches is in the spring when the leaves are just beginning to come out. They make a cool haze, a mist that seems to soften the stony hills of the Canadian shield.

In September, again, the birch leaves turn a purer gold than those of any other tree.

In 1764, Catherine the Great, desiring an impressive entrance to Siberia, had silver birches planted close together along both sides of the road east from Yekaterinburg. When these were full grown their branches met overhead, welcoming the wretched procession of exiles with a leafy tunnel over a hundred miles long, one of the great achievements in landscape architecture.

Landscaping can be an art form, and the birch is a valuable medium. It grows quickly and is more resistant than most lawn trees to disease and insects

Striking varieties have been brought to western lawns from Europe and Asia. None of these, to my mind, is better looking than the paper birch. Other birches, though, may be considered more spectacular or better adapted to warmer climates and to special requirements or landscape designs.

There is the common birch of Europe, *Betula pubescens*, and the more drooping silver birch, *Betula pendula*, of Scotland. Particularly graceful versions of the silver birch are the Swedish birch with deeply lobed leaves, the "Tristis" that soars and weeps, and Young's weeping birch with a low domed head and bare branches, all the foliage hanging down below them.

The colored-bark species are at their best in winter, when their glow shows warm against the snow. The southern white Chinese birch, *Betula albosinensis*, has pale reddish bark with a grayish bloom. The Himalayan birch, *Betula jaquemontii*, is variable in bark color, white to cream or brown.

The American gray birch (which is perfectly white with interesting dark marks at intervals on the trunk) forms clumps naturally. The river birch has beautifully colored bark in the fall and can grow in poorly drained soil. The Japanese *Betula japonica* has white bark. Both of these birches are pretty good at standing off the borer that kills paper birch in the central and southern United States.

> *Friends admire our many birch trees. These*
> *are birches, I tell them. We nod, chirpy as chipmunks,*
> *Until one says, OK, what kind of birches?*
> *Knowledge splits its subjects into chunks —*
>
> *that was years ago and still I study, beady-*
> *eyed, comparing catkin and leaf, double-toothed*
> *or lobed, searching for tufts of hair in vein*
> *axils, underneath, winged nuts, lambs' tails. The bark*
>
> *is ragged, shiny, pocked or peeling. Some smell*
> *like exotic dancers on Saturday night.*
> *In all seasons, leaves flutter on my bed,*
> *speaking Latin, contradictory. I know the song*

of names by now, seductive and misleading:
Cherry Birch   Blue Birch   Black Birch   Sweet;
River Birch   Red Birch   Water Birch   White;
Yellow, Paper, Silver, Downy, Gray

And the high Himalayan, though it's
Hard as hell to say just which is which.
And on the big one, warbling his ignorant head off,
Sits a goldfinch— some kind of a goldfinch.

"The Student," Peter Meinke

    I hold a freshly cut piece of birch bark in my hands. It is like a just-shot grouse or duck. The color has not yet begun to fade or the springy softness to stiffen. There is something wonderful here, something related to life.

    Wherever birches grow, all around the northern hemisphere, people from the earliest times must have had similar feelings. This smooth white sheet, conveniently at hand, light to carry, resistant to wear and rot, is just right for taking marks. It is like a sheet of fine watercolor paper. You feel the need to do something with it. From earliest times it must have been used for drawing and picture writing.

    The first art form was probably the transparency. That may have come many millennia before charcoal drawings, because charcoal requires fire. To make a transparency you need only a leaf or a piece of birch bark and your teeth.

    An Anishinaabekwe of my day peeled the outer bark into the thinnest possible sheets, warmed one of them at the fire, folded it (sometimes folding it several times), and bit the package. She would unfold it and hold it up to the light, revealing geometric designs, flowers, or human or animal figures. Everybody would give the quiet eu-eu sound to express wonder and applause.

Little girls would already be biting at scraps of bark, trying to get similar effects.

But the artist might see the possibility of improvement. Then she would fold and bite the bark again. She might fold the bark straight across or diagonally. Usually she bit with her eye teeth but sometimes with the premolars. She might twist the bark between her teeth. Sometimes she seemed to nibble at it. Each of these variations gave a different effect.

Eastern Indians may have developed this art even further than the Anishinaabeg. It is said that Montagnais women could produce bitten landscapes. The last survivor of the Beothuk, an old woman called Shanawdithit, or Nancy, died in 1829. She amazed her white captors with her bitten leaf and bark designs.

The Obugrians of western Siberia also bit designs into birch bark, but instead of piercing thin sheets with eye teeth they textured thicker sheets with the molars.

Nomads' art work must be portable and useful. You can't pack much in the way of paintings and statuary by reindeer, camel, or canoe. But the Lapp, Siberian, or North American artist was free to display her talents on light, strong necessities such as knife handles, net floats, and especially articles made of birch bark. Usually the art was of a sacred nature that would bring good hunting or fishing, or avert sickness.

The inner (cambium) surface of birch bark taken from the tree in late winter or early spring is of a reddish color. Designs were cut in this layer by scraping it away with a sharpened bone to show the lighter bark beneath. This was the principal means by which the American and Siberian tribal people decorated birch bark cups, pails and baskets. The Indians also used beads, porcupine and bird quills, spruce roots, sweet grass and moose hair.

A sharp tool of steel or bone makes a narrow hard-edged line, like an engraving, on the outer side of birch bark, or a deep, soft-edged groove on the cambium side.

The contrast in color between the inner and outer layers of bark was the basis for the technique used in most of the decorating of bowls, dishes and the basket-like boxes called makuks. The design might be made by scraping out the inner bark freehand, or by removing the cambium from around a cutout pattern.

Among the Montagnais, a decorated birch bark dish was sometimes given to a girl to bring her health and long life. A blessing might be inscribed on its bottom, just as was done in bowls by Semitic people of Asia Minor.

Decorated artifacts in present day museums no longer have this connection with the rituals and beliefs of their makers. By studying them and by reading and trying to understand those of the ancient stories that have been recorded, we may be able to sense some of the wisdom that we have lost a feeling for the infinite mystery around us.

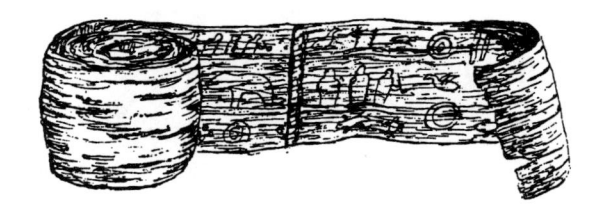

CHAPTER 10

WORLDS APART

Of my family, I, straying alone, am left behind.
The lakes where I used to fish have been left behind.
My tent poles are rotten.
My birch bark tent coverings are shriveled; they are gone.

Siberian lament

During the last hundred years, primitive Eurasian culture and tradition have disintegrated just as completely as has American Indian. Civilization has moved aggressively north on all three continents. Birch canoes have been replaced by motor boats, birch sledges and toboggans by snow machines, birch bark lodges by plastic houses, story-tellers by radio and television. Old legends, customs, languages and survival skills are dying with the few old men and women who remember them.

But the forest has suffered the most. Respect and even reverence for the tree has given way to the timber industry's motto "Cut out and get out."

The white man is not the only guilty party. Lapps and Siberians have readily joined the lunatic lunge toward "progress." Where the price was right, American Indians have opened silent lakes to motorboats and vast tracts of old growth forest to logging. People of all races have multiplied to pestilential numbers and are destroying the trees as grasshoppers destroy fields of grain. We have become a plague.

I don't want to sound too pious. I've done my share of damage with ax and brush hook. There is a Wagnerian ecstasy of conquest that can take hold of a farmer clearing land. Only my wife's determined intercession saved some fine old oaks that are still a delight now when our agricultural activities are over.

When I was a very young man I spent much time in logging camps. The management was generous to me and the men were friendly. So I have no feeling of hostility for the loggers and farmers who are doing the work.

But if a group of men were to enter the Louvre with chain saws and start cutting up the paintings, objections would be raised, no matter how pleasant and industrious the sawyers nor how badly they needed the jobs. The world is suffering a greater loss in the destruction of its forests.

Our principles of art, science, politics, religion and philosophy come to us, by way of European writers and teachers, from Asia Minor and Egypt through Greece and Rome. These ideas marched north with the Roman legions, sailed west with the conquistadors, jolted across the prairies in creaking Conestoga wagons, and galloped into Russia's Wild East with the Tsar's Cossacks. They overwhelmed the thoughts and beliefs of our ancestors of the taiga: Picts, Gaels, Germans, Scandinavians, Amerindians and Siberians. The forest people of Scotland and Germany could sometimes defeat the legions but they could not withstand the onslaught of Mediterranean civilization and religions. The ancient traditions of northern Europe were overwhelmed as completely as were, later, those of Siberia and North America.

These conquering ideas represented a rich culture for which we must all be grateful. But they originated with desert tribes to whom trees were suspected enemies. The forest was a hideous wilderness, a hideout for robbers, savages and evil spirits.

> *This savage forest, so dense and rugged,*
> *which even in memory renews my fear!*
> *The Inferno*, Dante

The leaves of cold forests withered in the heat of Mediterranean civilization and have blown away in the winds of time. The alliance between men and trees has been abrogated and denounced. Acid rain is destroying trees in areas protected from logging. The will and the power are at hand to bring about the final solution, in the Hitlerian sense, to the wilderness problem.

People all over the world are becoming aware of what is being done to the remnants of their forests. We are beginning to understand the wisdom of the old time reverence for trees. The birch tree still stands, a living presence, to remind us of times and places in which respect for nature was more important than the immediate pleasure and profit of the individual. The chain saws may yet be halted before all the masterpieces are cut down and paved over.

If this happens, we in the north can count on the birch, symbol of life, inception and rebirth, to lead the other trees back into the millennial process of restoration.

> *Spake the good old Wainamoinen:*
> *"Weep no longer, sacred birch tree,*
> *Mourn no more, my friend and brother,*
> *Thou shalt have a better fortune;*
> *Make thee laugh and sing with gladness."*
>
> *The Kalevala*

The artist listens to Ojibway tales—
tobacco for Ma-ni-do Gee-zhi-gance,
gifts offered at the spirit tree to calm
the great lake when the birch canoes set out.
All ships are frail, he thinks, all seas wild.

Witch Tree, Joanne Hart